# USBORNE SIMPLE READERS
# GOING SWIMMING

**Heather Amery**

**Illustrated by Peter Wingham**

**Reading Consultant: Betty Root**

Reading and Language Information Center
Reading University, England

This is Ben and Poppy.

This is Mom and Dad.

They have a cat called Cinders. And a dog called Punch.

2

Ben and Poppy have two friends called Clare and Tom.

They often play together. But sometimes they fight.

Today they are all going swimming.

They find their bathing suits and towels.
They look for their goggles, rings and armbands.

4

Dad puts everything into the car.
Cinders and Punch want to come too.

They drive to the swimming pool.
Punch has to stay in the car.

6

Dad buys the tickets.

The children go into the changing rooms.

Ben and Tom put on their bathing suits.

Then they put their clothes in the lockers.

Ben, Poppy, Clare and Tom are ready now.
They go to the pool.

Mom and Dad watch them from the side.

9

Poppy tries the water with her toes.

Tom can swim.
He jumps in.

Clare likes to walk down the ladder.

Ben can't swim.
He goes with Clare.

Poppy is learning to dive. She makes a big splash.

Poppy and Tom have a swimming race.
Who is going to win?

Tom likes jumping off
the diving board.

Poppy tries to teach Ben
to swim.

Clare has lots of turns
on the water slide.

They all have a game
with the ball.

Then Tom sees Punch. Dogs are not allowed in the swimming pool.

The life guard tries to catch Punch.
Dad chases him too.

Punch runs round the pool.  He thinks this is a game.

Punch runs past the tables.   He upsets one of them.

Everyone tries to catch Punch.
Dad nearly grabs him but misses.

Punch jumps into the water.
Dad slips on the wet floor and falls in.

Dad and Punch meet in the water.

Dad picks up Punch. Punch wants to swim again.

Poor Dad is very wet. He did not mean to go swimming.

Dad carries Punch up
the ladder.

And puts him down.
He is safe now.

Punch shakes himself.
He makes Mom wet too.

Mom puts a lead on Punch.
She takes him to the car.

Dad pulls off his wet coat
and shirt.

He takes off his shoes and
empties out the water.

He tries to wring out
his trousers.

He pulls out his pockets.
They are full of water.

Poppy and Tom are still playing in the pool.
Dad tells them to come out.

Dad helps Clare out.
She nearly falls in again.

Tom and Poppy climb out.
Mom comes back.

The boys go off to put
their clothes on.

First Tom has a shower.
He sprays Ben with water.

While the boys dress,
they play hide-and-seek.

Dad is still very wet.
He tries on Tom's tee-shirt.

Mom goes with Clare and Poppy to change.

Mom helps Clare on with her clothes.

Mom brushes Poppy's hair. Clare puts on her shoes.

They pack up their wet swimming things.

21

They all meet outside the changing rooms.
Everyone wants an ice cream or a drink.

They have to wait for Clare.
She has forgotten her towel.

She goes back to the
changing room.

22

They all go to the café.
Everyone wants something different.

Dad counts out his wet money.
What did they choose to eat and drink?

23

They drive home in the car.
And Dad can put on some dry clothes.

First published in 1986. Usborne Publishing Ltd, 20 Garrick Street, London WC2E 9BJ, England. © Usborne Publishing Ltd, 1986.